READING/WRITING COMPANION

Mc
Graw
Hill
Education

Cover: Nathan Love, Erwin Madrid

mheducation.com/prek-12

Send all inquiries to:
McGraw-Hill Education
Two Penn Plaza
New York, NY 10121

ISBN: 978-0-07-902063-5
MHID: 0-07-902063-1

Printed in the United States of America.

4 5 6 7 8 9 LMN 23 22 21 20   C

Welcome to Wonders!

Explore exciting **Literature**, **Science**, and **Social Studies** texts!

★ **READ** about the world around you!

★ **THINK**, **SPEAK**, and **WRITE** about genres!

★ **COLLABORATE** in discussions and inquiry!

★ **EXPRESS** yourself!

my.mheducation.com

Use your student login to read texts and practice phonics, spelling, grammar, and more!

Unit 9 How Things Change

The Big Idea

Week 1 • Growing Up

Digital Tools Find this eBook and other resources at: my.mheducation.com

Week 2 • Good Citizens

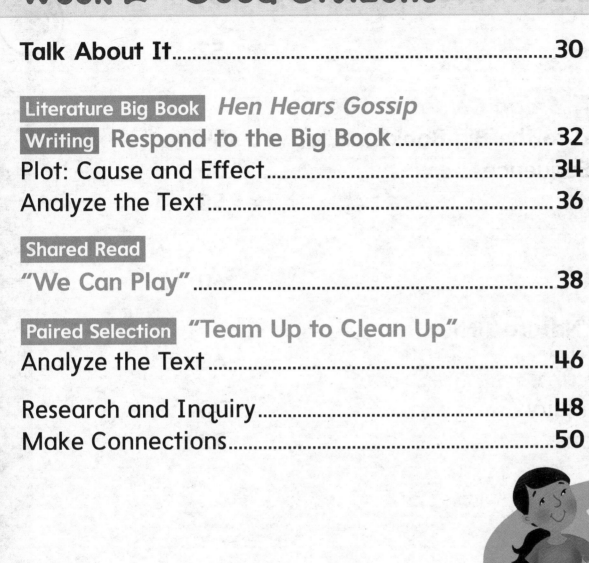

Week 3 · Our Natural Resources

SOCIAL STUDIES

How Things Change

The Big Idea

How do things change?

Talk about how the caterpillar changes in the photos. Answer any questions your partner may have about your ideas.

Draw a picture of a butterfly.

Talk About It

Talk about how this boy helps out at home.

 Write about one way you help out at home.

_____

_____

_____

_____

_____

_____

_____

_____

Retell the realistic fiction story.

 Write about the story.

What is this story mostly about?

_____

- -

_____

🔍 **Text Evidence**

Page

How do you know it is realistic fiction?

_____

- -

_____

🔍 **Text Evidence**

Page

- -

_____

Talk about how children can help with a new baby.

 Write about one way children can help with a new baby.

Children can help by

_____

_____

Make Inferences

The **theme** of a story can be the message or lesson it tells. Talk about why Peter helps paint his chair pink. How does this help you understand the theme of this story?

The events in a story are called the plot.
The plot has a <u>beginning</u>, a <u>middle</u>,
and an <u>end</u>.

 Listen to the story.

 Talk about the plot. What happens
in the **beginning, middle,** and **end**?

 Write about what happens.

Quick Tip

Was there a part
of the story
that you did not
understand? How did
what you already
know about the topic
of the story help you?

Beginning

Middle

End

Listen to and **look** at pages 6–7.

 Talk about clues the author gives that help you know how Peter feels.

 Write and **draw** clues in the chart.

Word clues	Picture clues

How does Peter feel?

_____

- -

_____

Listen to and **look** at pages 16–19.

 Talk about things that are important
to Peter. How does the author let you know?

 Draw and **label** them.

Find Text Evidence

 Read the title. Look at the picture. Think about what you want to find out in this story.

Circle and read the word **too**.

Jake and Dale Help!

Jake and Dale wake up.

Jake can make a bed.

Dale can make a bed, too.

Find Text Evidence

 Read and point to each sentence. Be sure to read from the top of each page to the bottom. Be sure to read from left to right.

 Circle and read the word **help**.

"Can you help?" said Dad.

Dale can get a tan cup.

Jake can get the red jam.

Jake can take Rex.

Dale can take Rex, too.

Run, run Rex to the lake!

Shared Read

🔍 **Find Text Evidence**

Ask questions you may have as you read. Read to find the answers.

Circle the word **rake**. Also circle the rake in the picture.

Jake and Dale help Dad.

Jake can wax a big van.

Dale can rake, rake, rake!

Dale and Jake help Mom.

They get in a big van.

A big van can go, go, go!

Shared Read

🔍 **Find Text Evidence**

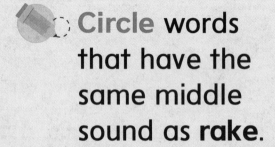

Circle words that have the same middle sound as **rake**.

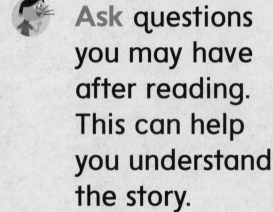

Ask questions you may have after reading. This can help you understand the story. Then retell the story.

Mom can get a big, big sack.

Dale can get a big yam.

Jake can get a cake mix.

Jake, Dale, and Mom bake.

They can bake a quick cake.

Dale and Jake help a lot!

Listen to and **look** at the play.
How do people in this family help out?

 Draw a box around each character in the play.

 Circle the narrator.

Meet the Characters

Mom

Dad

Juan

Ana

Narrator

Quick Tip

- A **drama**, or play, is a story told by characters who talk to each other.

- The **narrator** tells details about what happens in the play.

Listen to and **look** at page 34.

 Talk and **write** about how the characters say they can help Mom.

Talk About It

What are some differences between a play and a story?

Character	What the character says

How to Help Out at Home

Step 1 **Talk** about different ways children can help out at home.

Step 2 **Write** questions about ways children can help out at home.

_____

- - - - - - - - - - - - - - - - - -

_____

_____

- - - - - - - - - - - - - - - - - -

_____

Step 3 **Interview** three classmates. Ask them your questions.

Step 4 **List** different ways your classmates said that they can help out at home.

_____

- -

_____

_____

_____

- -

_____

_____

- -

_____

Step 5 **Choose** a good way to present your work.

My Grandma Says

My grandma says
I know you are able
To set the table,
To help me
bake bread,

Or make a bed.
But now, the very best
Thing you can do
Is to sit on my lap
And just be you.

 Listen to the poem.

 Compare the child in the poem to Peter in *Peter's Chair*.

 Talk about how the poem and the story show that these children are growing up.

Quick Tip

We can ask and answer questions before, during, and after reading. This helps us understand what we read and learn new information.

What I Know Now

Think about the texts you read this week.

The texts tell about

_____

- -

_____

_____

- -

_____

 Think about what you learned this week.
What else would you like to learn?
Talk about your ideas.

 Share one thing you learned about
realistic fiction stories.

Talk About It

Essential Question What do good citizens do?

Talk about how these children are being good citizens.

Write about being a good citizen.

A good citizen is someone who

_____

- -

_____

_____

- -

_____

One way I can be a good citizen is

_____

- -

_____

Retell the fantasy story.

 Write about the fantasy.

Why does Hen try to hear what Cow whispers to Pig?

_____

- -

_____

Text Evidence

Page

Why does Duck say that the cat grew a horn?

_____

- -

_____

- -

_____

Text Evidence

Page

Talk about what can happen when people do not listen carefully.

Write about what can happen.

_____

- -

_____

_____

- -

_____

_____

- -

_____

A cause is what makes something happen.
An effect is the event that happens.

 Listen carefully to part of the story.

 Talk about the causes and effects in the story.

 Write the causes and effects.

Combine Information

In this story, many animals tell what they think happened.

How does what Cow says on page 24 change your understanding?

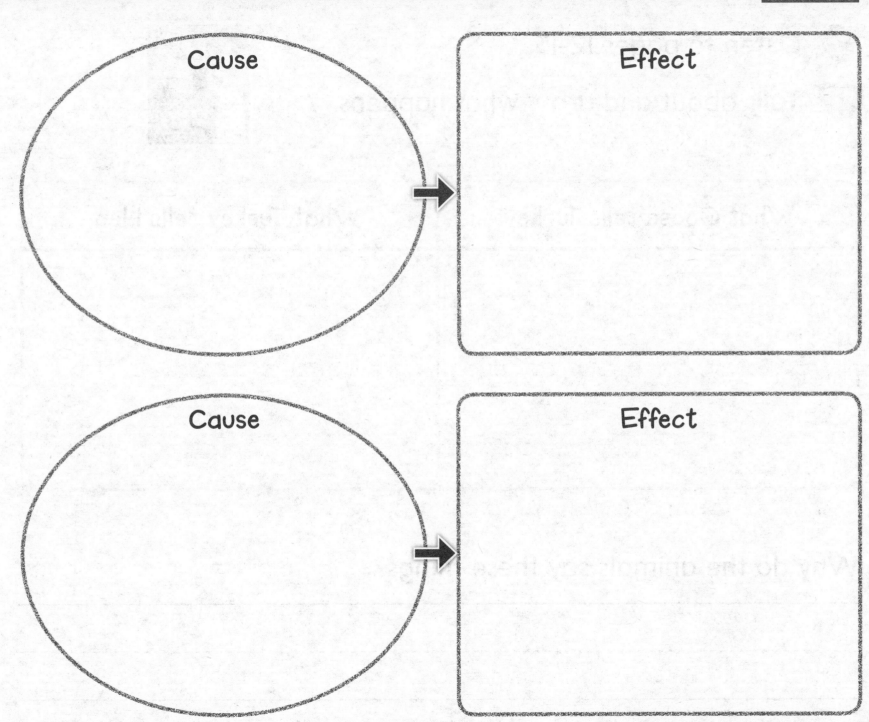

Cause

Effect

Cause

Effect

 Listen to pages 12–15.

 Talk about and draw what happens.

What Goose tells Turkey	What Turkey tells Hen

Why do the animals say these things?

_____

- -

_____

Look at page 15.

 Talk about why the author uses uppercase letters in some words.

 Draw and **write** about how Hen feels.

Hen feels

_____

- -

_____

Find Text Evidence

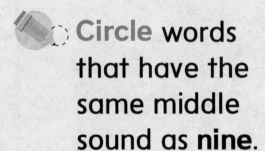 Read the title. Look at the picture. Think about what you want to find out in this story.

Circle words that have the same middle sound as **nine**.

We Can Play

Mike can ride a red bike.

Kate can ride a tan bike.

They ride in a bike lane.

Shared Read

🔍 **Find Text Evidence**

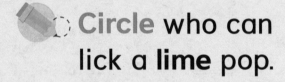 **Underline** words that have the same middle sound as **five**.

Circle who can lick a **lime** pop.

Mike is in a line.

Mike can let Pam in.

Pam can get in the line.

Pam can lick a red pop.

Mike can lick a lime pop.

Kate can get a big cup.

Shared Read

🔍 **Find Text Evidence**

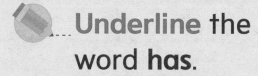 **Underline** the word **has**.

 **Circle** the picture whose name rhymes with **bite**. Also circle the word.

Mike has a fine red bike.

"It is mine," said Mike.

"But Pam can take a ride!"

Kate and Pam have a kite.

It can go up, up a mile!

Mike can let it go up, too.

Shared Read

 Find Text Evidence

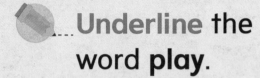 Underline the word **play**.

Look at the pictures for clues if you do not understand something. Then retell the story.

Kate and Pam play a game.

They run a lot and kick.

The game is quite fun!

Pam can see Mike.

"You can play," said Pam.

They have a fun time.

Look at the photos. How are these children being good citizens?

 Talk and **write** about what these children are doing.

What will happen to the plastic bottles? How do you know?

_____

- -

_____

- -

_____

Listen to these sentences. How do these children feel about cleaning up?

 Underline clues in the words and caption.

 Circle clues in the photo.

We took responsibility for making our neighborhood an even better place!

We did a good job!

©Ariel Skelley/Blend Images/Getty Images

How to Be a Good Citizen

Step 1 Talk about things good citizens do.

Step 2 Write questions about being
a good citizen.

_____

- -

_____

_____

- -

_____

Step 3 Interview school workers and students.
Ask them your questions.

Step 4 Write what you learned in the chart.

Name	Idea about how to be a good citizen

Step 5 Choose a good way to present your work.

Talk about the art. How was Paul Revere a good citizen?

 Compare this art to "Team Up to Clean Up." What do the art and this text tell about what good citizens do?

Quick Tip

We can look at art to learn information.

Paul Revere lived more than 200 years ago.
He warned his town that British soldiers were coming.

National Archives and Records Administration (NWDNS-208-FS-3200-5)

What I Know Now

Think about the texts you read this week.

The texts tell about

_____

- -

_____

- -

_____

 Think about what you learned this week.
What else would you like to learn?
Talk about your ideas.

 Share one thing you learned
about fantasy stories.

Talk About It

Essential Question How can things in nature be used to make new things?

Talk about what this girl is making from the oranges.

 Write the name of another fruit or vegetable in the top oval. Write what you can make with it in the other ovals.

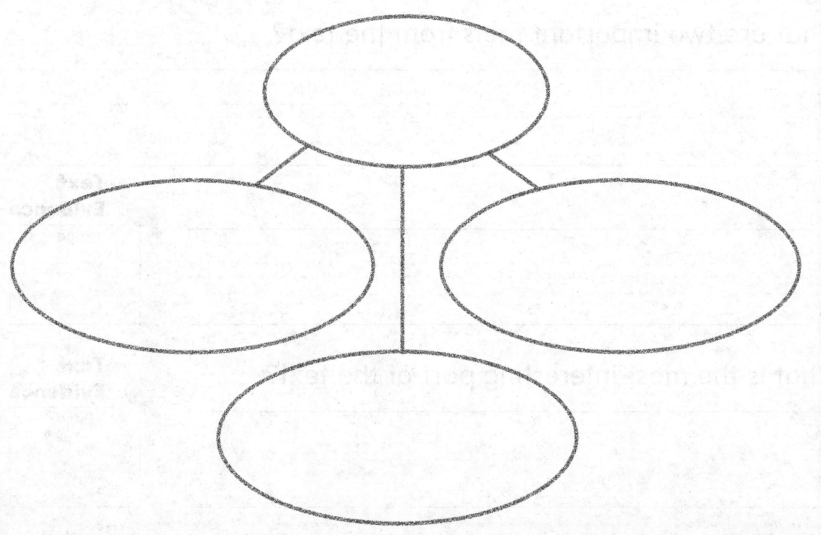

Read | Respond to the Big Book

 Retell the nonfiction text.

 Write about the text. Use new words you learned.

What are two important facts from the text?

1. _____

Text Evidence
Page

2. _____

What is the most interesting part of the text?

_____

Text Evidence
Page

Talk about foods in your store that are made from grain.

Write a list of these foods.

Nonfiction text can tell information in sequence. Sequence is the order in which events happen.

 Listen to part of the text.

 Talk about what happens **first, next,** and **last.**

 Write about what happens.

Quick Tip

Sometimes when we read, we do not understand parts of the text. When this happens, we can think about what we already know about the topic.

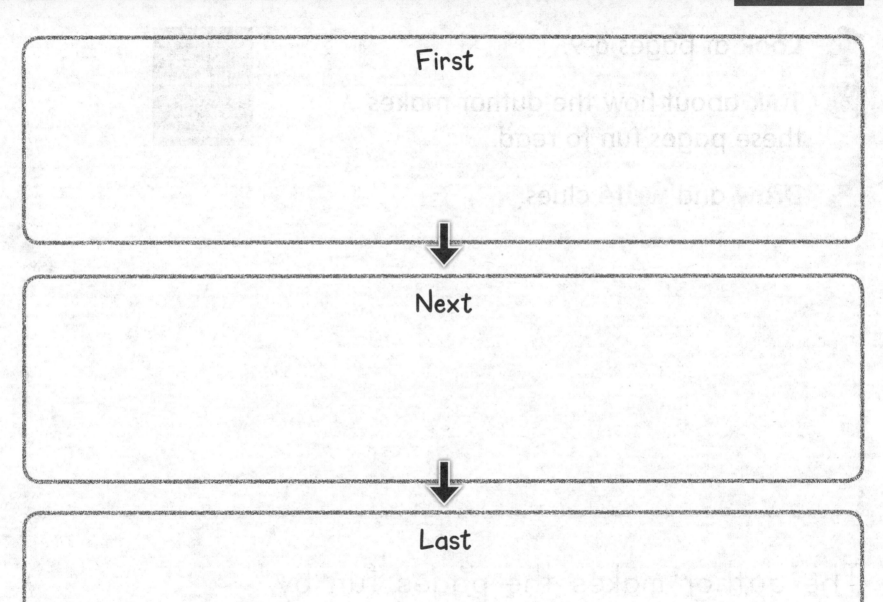

First

Next

Last

Look at pages 6–9.

 Talk about how the author makes these pages fun to read.

 Draw and **write** clues.

The author makes the pages fun by

_____

- -

_____

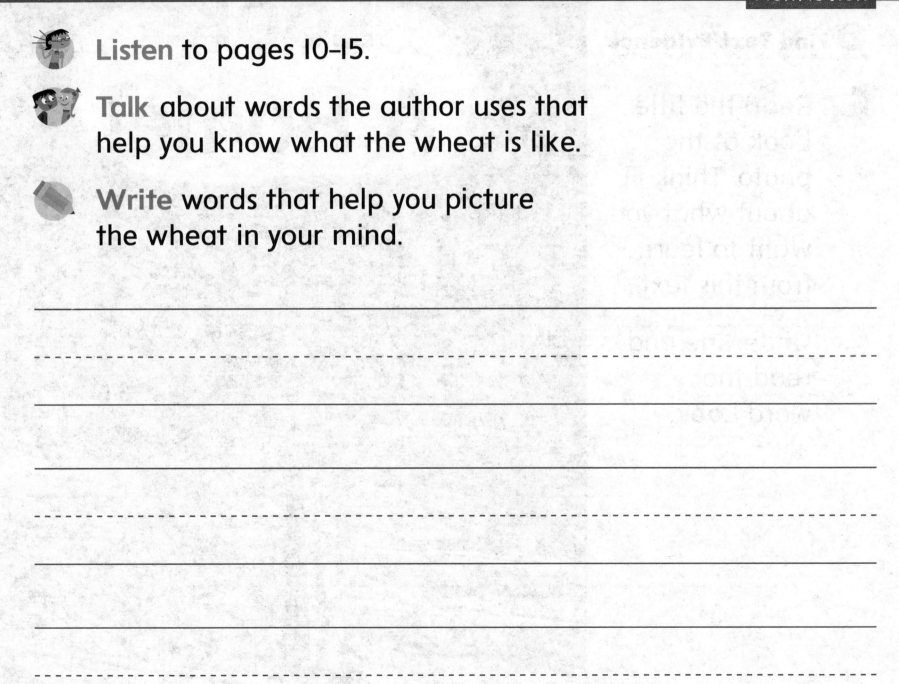

Listen to pages 10–15.

Talk about words the author uses that help you know what the wheat is like.

Write words that help you picture the wheat in your mind.

🔍 Find Text Evidence

 Read the title. Look at the photo. Think about what you want to learn from this text.

Underline and read the word **Look**.

Look! A Home!

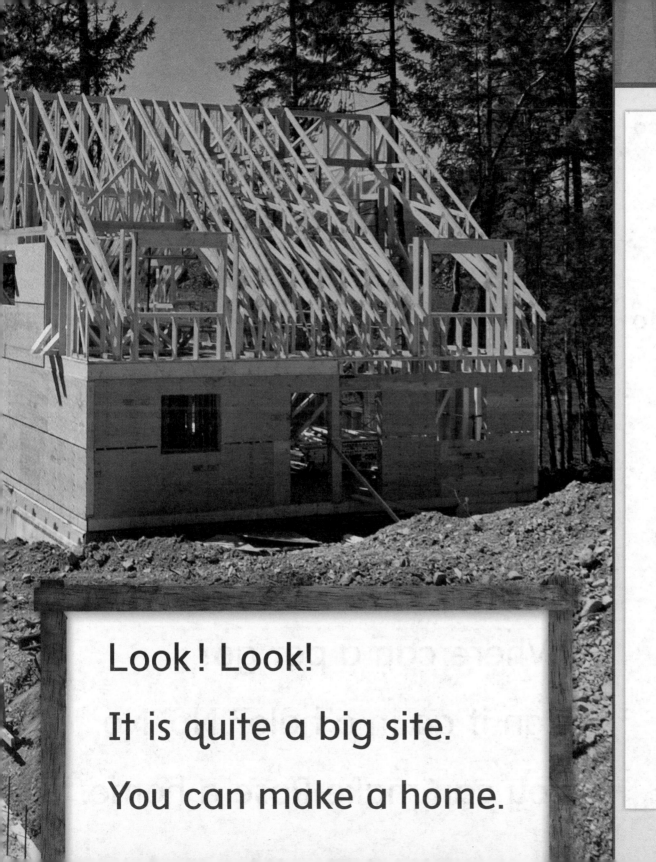

Look! Look!

It is quite a big site.

You can make a home.

Shared Read

🔍 **Find Text Evidence**

✏️ **Underline** and read the word **Where**.

✏️ **Circle** the photo of the **bone**. Also circle the word. Then circle other words that have the same middle sound.

Where can a pet go?

Can it go in a hole? No. No.

You can make Rose a home.

(t)Comstock/Getty Images; (frame)C Squared Studios/SuperStock

Cole can sit in a fine home.

Cole can bite a big bone.

Yum! Yum! Yum! Yum!

Find Text Evidence

 Read from the top of each page to the bottom. Be sure to read from left to right. When you get to the end of a line, go to the first word in the next line.

 Circle the word **pole**.

This is not a pet.

But we can make it a home.

It is safe in a home!

This is quite fine, too.

It is on a big, big pole.

I bet you can make it.

Shared Read

 Circle a **rope** on page 67.

Ask questions if you do not understand something. Reread to find the answers. Then retell the text.

This is a big, fine home.

It can take a lot of time!

But it is a fun, fun job.

(t)Palabra/Alamy; (frame)C Squared Studios/SuperStock

Look what you can make!

Sit on it and go up, up, up.

You can have a lot of fun.

I hope you like it!

Listen to part of the text.
Look at the photos. What kinds
of art can people make using
things from nature?

Circle the sculptor carving a mask.

Draw a box around the artist
weaving a rug.

(l)David Lyons/Alamy Stock Photo; (c)Patrick J. Endres/Corbis Documentary/Getty Images; (r)Paul Chesley/The Image Bank/Getty Images

Talk and **write** about the things from nature that these artists use.

What does the sculptor use to carve a mask?

_____

- -

_____

What does the artist use to weave a basket?

_____

- -

_____

What does the artist use to weave a rug?

_____

- -

_____

Talk About It

Look at pages 34–35. How does the author use photos and captions to tell more about making pottery?

Products from Trees

Step 1 Talk about how trees are used
to make different products.
Choose one kind of tree to learn about.

Step 2 Write questions about products that
are made from this tree.

_____

- -

_____

- -

_____

Step 3 Look at books or use the Internet.
Look up words you do not know.
Use a picture or online dictionary.

Step 4 Write about what you learned.

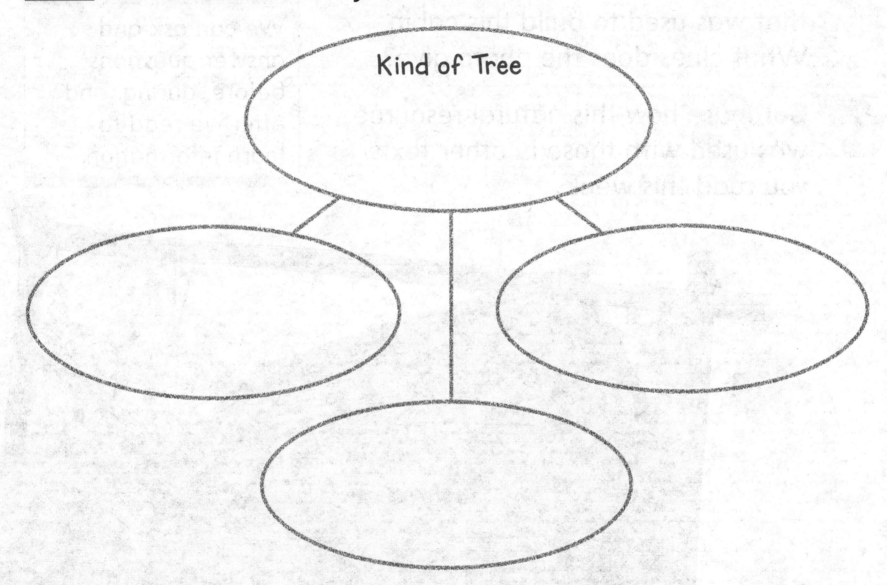

Kind of Tree

Step 5 Choose a good way to present your work.

Think about a natural resource that was used to build this cabin. What clues does the photo give?

 Compare how this natural resource was used with those in other texts you read this week.

Quick Tip

We can ask and answer questions before, during, and after we read to learn information.

What I Know Now

Think about the texts you read this week.

The texts tell about

_____

_____

_____

_____

_____

 Think about what you learned this week.
What else would you like to learn?
Talk about your ideas.

 Share one thing you learned
about nonfiction texts.

My Sound-Spellings

Aa a apple	**Bb** b bat	**Cc** c ck k camel	**Dd** d dolphin	**Ee** e egg	**Ff** f fire	**Gg** g guitar
Hh h_ hippo	**Ii** i insect	**Jj** j jump	**Kk** c k ck koala	**Ll** l lemon	**Mm** m map	**Nn** n nest
Oo o octopus	**Pp** p piano	**Qq** qu_ queen	**Rr** r rose	**Ss** s sun	**Tt** t turtle	**Uu** u umbrella
Vv v volcano	**Ww** w_ window	**Xx** x box	**Yy** y_ yo-yo	**Zz** z _s zipper		

Aa Bb Cc Dd Ee

Ff Gg Hh Ii Jj

Kk Ll Mm Nn

Oo Pp Qq Rr

Ss Tt Uu Vv

Ww Xx Yy Zz